20 FUN FACTS ABOUT THE GRAND CANYON

BY EMILY MAHONEY

Gareth Stevens
PUBLISHING

Please visit our website, www.garethstevens.com. For a free color catalog of all our high-quality books, call toll free 1-800-542-2595 or fax 1-877-542-2596.

Cataloging-in-Publication Data

Names: Mahoney, Emily.
Title: 20 fun facts about the Grand Canyon / Emily Mahoney.
Description: New York : Gareth Stevens Publishing, 2020. | Series: Fun fact file: world wonders! | Includes glossary and index.
Identifiers: ISBN 9781538237700 (pbk.) | ISBN 9781538237724 (library bound) | ISBN 9781538237717 (6 pack)
Subjects: LCSH: Grand Canyon National Park (Ariz.)–Juvenile literature. | National parks and reserves–Arizona–Juvenile literature.
Classification: LCC F788.M32 2019 | DDC 979.1'32–dc23

First Edition

Published in 2020 by
Gareth Stevens Publishing
111 East 14th Street, Suite 349
New York, NY 10003

Copyright © 2020 Gareth Stevens Publishing

Designer: Sarah Liddell
Editor: Kristen Nelson

Photo credits: Cover, p. 1 Jon Chica/Shutterstock.com; file folder used throughout David Smart/Shutterstock.com; binder clip used throughout luckyraccoon/Shutterstock.com; wood grain background used throughout ARENA Creative/Shutterstock.com; p. 5 TheBigMK/Shutterstock.com; p. 6 DEA/L. ROMANO/Contributor/De Agostini/Getty Images; p. 7 kojihirano/Shutterstock.com; p. 8 Space Frontiers/Stringer/Archive Photos/Getty Images; p. 9 Iulia Nagy Photography/Shutterstock.com; p. 10 Everett Historical/Shutterstock.com; p. 11 Globe Turner/Shutterstock.com; p. 12 Maridav/Shutterstock.com; p. 13 Daniel Harwardt/Shutterstock.com; p. 14 Ralph Lee Hopkins/Lonely Planet Images/Getty Images; p. 15 Christine Gibson/Contributor/Moment/Getty Images; p. 16 Boris15/Shutterstock.com; p. 17 Robin Skjoldborg/Contributor/Getty Images; p. 18 Education Images/Contributor/Universal Images Group/Getty Images; p. 19 James Marvin Phelps/Shutterstock.com; p. 20 albertczyzewski/Shutterstock.com; p. 21 Fredlyfish4/Shutterstock.com; p. 22 Skreidzeleu/Shutterstock.com; p. 23 ronnybas frimages/Shutterstock.com; p. 24 nootprapa/Shutterstock.com; p. 25 (hiking) Galyna Andrushko/Shutterstock.com; p. 25 (skydiving) Mauricio Graiki/Shutterstock.com; p. 25 (white water rafting) Elena Arrigo/Shutterstock.com; p. 25 (fishing) Ray Redstone/Shutterstock.com; p. 26 Wolfgang Kaehler/Contributor/LightRocket/Getty Images; p. 27 Tim Boyles/Contributor/Getty Images Entertainment/Getty Images; p. 29 Erik Harrison/Shutterstock.com.

Printed in the United States of Americ

CPSIA compliance information: Batch #CS19GS: For further information contact Gareth Stevens, New York, New York at 1-800-542-2595.

CONTENTS

Words in the glossary appear in **bold** type the first time they are used in the text.

A NATURAL WONDER

The Grand Canyon is one of the most beautiful naturally created places in the world. Its large size, depth, and amazing rock formations wow millions of people who visit it each year.

But how did the Grand Canyon form? And just how deep is it? The answers to these questions, as well as many more fun facts, can be found right here. Keep reading to learn all about this world wonder: the Grand Canyon!

The Grand Canyon is often called one of the seven natural wonders of the world.

A HUGE CANYON

THE GRAND CANYON'S LENGTH IS ABOUT 50 TIMES THE HEIGHT OF MOUNT EVEREST.

The Grand Canyon is 277 miles (446 km) long. If you drove a car at 60 miles (96.6 km) per hour, it would take you more than 4 1/2 hours to drive the length of the Grand Canyon!

A canyon is a deep valley with tall sides of rock. There's often a river flowing through it. The Colorado River flows through the Grand Canyon.

6

THE GRAND CANYON'S DEEPEST POINT IS ABOUT 6,000 FEET (1,829 M)!

You could fit about four Empire State Buildings stacked on top of each other in that part of the Grand Canyon! But the Grand Canyon isn't this deep its whole length.

DIFFERENT PARTS OF THE CANYON ARE DIFFERENT WIDTHS ACROSS.

At its widest point, the Grand Canyon is 18 miles (29 km) rim to rim. This measurement doesn't make it the widest canyon on Earth. That's Capertree Valley in Australia, which is slightly wider.

The Grand Canyon is so big, it can be seen from space!

AT ITS NARROWEST POINT, THE GRAND CANYON IS ONLY 1,800 FEET (549 M) ACROSS.

This narrow point is in Marble Canyon. It became recognized as part of Grand Canyon National Park in 1975 when President Gerald Ford signed the Grand Canyon Enlargement Act to protect more land in the area.

NATIONALLY KNOWN

THE GRAND CANYON BECAME A NATIONAL PARK IN 1919.

President Theodore Roosevelt, who was **passionate** about the outdoors, made the canyon a national monument in January 1908. This was to protect, or keep safe, the area's natural beauty for the future. This led to it becoming a national park.

It was very important to President Roosevelt that the canyon was protected from people wanting to build in or near it.

WHERE IS GRAND CANYON NATIONAL PARK?

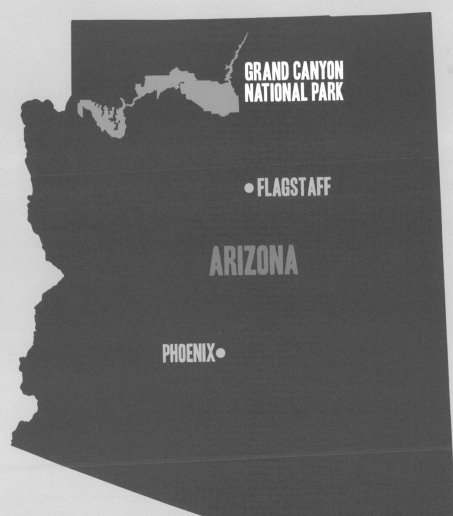

GRAND CANYON NATIONAL PARK

●FLAGSTAFF

ARIZONA

PHOENIX●

Grand Canyon National Park is found in northern Arizona, north of the city of Flagstaff.

It's important to carry a map when traveling through this large park.

GRAND CANYON NATIONAL PARK COVERS MORE THAN 1 MILLION ACRES (404,686 HA) OF LAND.

Since it's so large, visitors can't see the entire park in 1 day.

They often choose to visit parts of the canyon such as the South

Rim, Grand Canyon West, Grand Canyon East, or the North Rim.

FORMING A CANYON

THE GRAND CANYON HAS BEEN FORMING FOR MILLIONS OF YEARS.

As the water from the Colorado River continues to erode the layers of rock, the canyon's twists and turns change.

The Colorado River running through the Grand Canyon is the main force behind **eroding** the rock that makes up the canyon. Wind erosion has also played a part in the canyon's formation.

13

The **volcanoes** in the Grand Canyon haven't erupted in about 10,000 years. You can still visit an ancient volcano called Vulcan's Throne.

THERE ARE VOLCANOES IN THE GRAND CANYON!

About 630,000 years ago, volcanic **eruptions** began in what's now the Grand Canyon. The lava blocked the Colorado River from flowing. The river eventually broke through these places and wore away a path.

FIRST FOOTSTEPS IN THE CANYON

PEOPLE HAVE LIVED IN THE GRAND CANYON FOR HUNDREDS OF YEARS!

The Havasupai have lived in and around the Grand Canyon for 800 years. Today, their **reservation** is located 8 miles (12.9 km) down in the canyon, and you can't get there by road. All their mail is delivered by pack mule!

A man named John Powell led a group of explorers through the canyon in 1869. They had a difficult journey because one of their boats sank and much of their food went bad.

THE FIRST OFFICIAL AMERICAN EXPLORER OF THE CANYON CALLED IT "VALUELESS."

An army officer named Joseph Christmas Ives traveled up the Colorado River by boat in 1857. He thought the area was "astounding" but that "after entering it there is nothing to do but leave."

NATURE IN THE GRAND CANYON

THE WEATHER IN THE GRAND CANYON VARIES FROM LOCATION TO LOCATION.

Before you hike in the Grand Canyon, it's a good idea to check the weather. You don't want to be too hot or cold!

During the summer, the temperature can be over 100°F (37.7°C) on the canyon's South Rim, but only about 70°F (21°C) on the North Rim. Overnight temperatures on the North Rim during the summer sometimes drop below freezing!

THERE ARE OVER 1,500 KINDS OF PLANTS IN GRAND CANYON NATIONAL PARK.

Some of these plants **thrive** with very little water, whereas others need lots of water to survive. The Grand Canyon has both, with **habitats** ranging from desert to forest.

Bighorn sheep are some of the largest animals to live around the Grand Canyon.

ABOUT 355 BIRD SPECIES LIVE IN AND AROUND THE GRAND CANYON.

There are also about 90 kinds of **mammals**, more than 40 kinds of **reptiles**, 9 kinds of amphibians, and 17 kinds of fish. If you were to visit, you might see a squirrel, a spiny lizard, a bighorn sheep, and even a mountain lion!

MORE THAN 5 MILLION PEOPLE VISIT THE GRAND CANYON EVERY YEAR.

When the park first opened in 1919, only about 44,000 people visited. Now, people come from all over the world for the breathtaking views or to take part in fun outdoor activities.

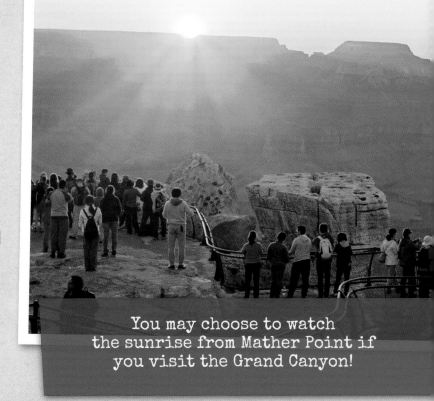

You may choose to watch the sunrise from Mather Point if you visit the Grand Canyon!

Some people who hike rim to rim stay overnight in the canyon at Phantom Ranch.

EACH YEAR, LESS THAN 1 PERCENT OF GRAND CANYON VISITORS HIKE FROM THE NORTH RIM TO THE SOUTH RIM.

While there is a road around the canyon about 212 miles (341 km) long, some people want the challenge of hiking rim to rim instead! This hike is about 24 miles (36 km) of hard climbing and walking.

MORE PEOPLE HAVE BEEN ON THE MOON THAN HIKED THE GRAND CANYON END TO END IN ONE TRIP.

As of 2017, only eight people had finished the 800-mile (1,287 km) hike all at once. Only around 26 had hiked the whole canyon in a few trips.

THE GRAND CANYON IS HOME TO A WATERFALL.

It's a hard, 10-mile (16 km) hike to get to Havasu Falls, found on the Havasupai Indian Reservation. In fact, the hike is so hard that you'll have to spend the night camping nearby should you choose to make the trip.

YOU CAN WALK 4,000 FEET (1,219 M) ABOVE THE GRAND CANYON!

The Skywalk is a glass-bottomed, horseshoe-shaped bridge that sticks out 70 feet (21.3 m) from the canyon's edge. If you're brave, you can look down through the glass floor to the bottom!

The Skywalk is found at Eagle Point.

FUN AT THE GRAND CANYON

SKYDIVING
THOSE WHO SEE THE GRAND CANYON WHILE SKYDIVING CAN REACH SPEEDS OF MORE THAN 120 MILES (193 KM) PER HOUR!

HIKING
VISITORS CAN TAKE SHORT HIKES OF JUST A FEW MILES OR EVEN HIKE FOR DAYS IN THE GRAND CANYON!

WHITE WATER RAFTING
YOU CAN SPEND ALMOST 2 WEEKS ON YOUR RAFT TRAVELING DOWN THE MIGHTY COLORADO RIVER!

FISHING
YOU NEED A PERMIT, OR A PAPER GIVING YOU PERMISSION, TO FISH IN THE GRAND CANYON. THE BEST TIME TO FISH THERE IS IN FALL AND WINTER!

DANGEROUS YET BEAUTIFUL

YOU HAVE A 1 IN 400,000 CHANCE OF DYING WHILE VISITING THE GRAND CANYON.

People have died in the canyon from the heat, **dehydration**, car crashes—and falling over the rim. This doesn't mean you shouldn't visit though. Just be careful when you try to take that cool photo!

A spokesperson from Grand Canyon National Park said they won't allow events that might interrupt visitors or the peacefulness of the park. A tightrope walk may have done that!

A TIGHTROPE WALKER CROSSED THE GRAND CANYON IN 2013—OR DID HE?

Tightrope walker Nik Wallenda was reported in the news as walking across the Grand Canyon. But he didn't! The park wouldn't allow him to. He walked across the nearby Little Colorado River Gorge.

PROTECTING THE CANYON

A trip to the Grand Canyon allows you to see amazing wildlife and enjoy the scenic paths through different areas of the canyon. You can even take a helicopter ride through it!

The Grand Canyon must be taken care of so people in the future can take part in everything this beautiful area has to offer. If you're able to visit the Grand Canyon, be sure to leave things the way you found them so others can enjoy this natural wonder!

Maybe you will be one of
the 5 million people to visit
the Grand Canyon this year!

GLOSSARY

dehydration: to have lost too much water from the body

erode: to wear away outer layers of rock or soil by the action of wind, water, or ice

eruption: a bursting forth

habitat: the place or type of place where a plant or animal naturally or normally lives or grows

mammal: a warm-blooded animal that has a backbone and hair, breathes air, and feeds milk to its young

passionate: showing great emotion

reptile: an animal covered with scales or plates that breathes air, has a backbone, and lays eggs, such as a turtle, snake, lizard, or crocodile

reservation: land set aside by the US government for Native Americans

species: a group of plants or animals that are all of the same kind

thrive: to grow or develop successfully

vary: to be different or to become different

volcano: an opening in a planet's surface through which hot, liquid rock sometimes flows

FOR MORE INFORMATION

BOOKS

Chin, Jason. *Grand Canyon*. New York, NY: Roaring Brook Press, 2017.

Mattern, Joanne. *The Grand Canyon: This Place Rocks*. South Egremont, MA: Red Chair Press, 2018.

O'Connor, Jim. *Where Is the Grand Canyon?* New York, NY: Grosset & Dunlap, 2015.

WEBSITES

Grand Canyon National Park
kids.nationalgeographic.com/explore/nature/grand-canyon/ #GrandCanyonlandscape.jpg
Explore facts and see amazing pictures of the Grand Canyon on National Geographic's kids' site.

Grand Canyon: Water Erosion
kidsgeo.com/geology-for-kids/grand-canyon/
Learn about the geology of the Grand Canyon here.

Kids and Rangers: Grand Canyon National Park
www.nps.gov/grca/learn/kidsyouth/index.htm
The National Park Service hosts this website with kid-friendly information about Grand Canyon National Park.

INDEX